PASTA

40 WONDERFUL CLASSIC PASTA RECIPES

This is a Parragon Publishing Book
This edition published in 2006

Parragon Publishing
Queen Street House
4 Queen Street
Bath BA1 1HE, UK

ISBN: 1-40547-420-3

Printed in China

Design concept by Fiona Roberts
Produced by the Bridgewater Book Company Ltd

Notes for the Reader

This book uses imperial, metric, or US cup measurements. Follow the same units of measurement throughout; do not mix imperial and metric. All spoon measurements are level: teaspoons are assumed to be 5 ml, and tablespoons are assumed to be 15 ml. Unless otherwise stated, milk is assumed to be whole, eggs and individual vegetables such as potatoes are medium, and pepper is freshly ground black pepper. Recipes using raw or very lightly cooked eggs should be avoided by infants, the elderly, pregnant women, convalescents, and anyone suffering from an illness.

Introduction

There is surely no other food that could be simpler. Pasta,the national dish of Italy is now eaten all over the world. It is made from durum wheat flour and water, and sometimes enriched with egg or oil. Although it may be one of the simplest of foods, it is probably the most varied. It comes in over 650 different shapes and sizes, and can be flavored by herbs, spinach, or tomato. Pasta can be prepared by hand or in a food processor. When cooking, the secrets of success are to cook it in the largest pan available, and make sure the water is boiling when you add the pasta. Cook at a rolling boil, and don't overdrain it. Whatever you do, don't rinse the pasta and never overcook it as it will be soft and mushy—*al dente* (firm to the bite) is the best result. On that note, try these easy recipes and enjoy the delicious dishes they make.

Basic recipes

BASIC PASTA DOUGH

This is the most basic recipe for making pasta dough by hand or using a food processor. You can add colorings and flavorings according to the dish (see right).

SERVES 3–4

1 1/3 cups white all-purpose flour or white bread flour, plus extra for dusting
pinch of salt
2 eggs, lightly beaten
1 tbsp olive oil

• To make the pasta dough by hand, sift the flour and salt onto a clean counter and make a well in the center. Pour the eggs and oil into the well, then using your fingers, gradually combine them and incorporate the flour.

• Turn out the dough onto a lightly floured counter and knead until smooth. Wrap the dough in plastic wrap and let rest for at least 30 minutes before rolling out or feeding through a pasta machine, as this makes it more elastic. Use as required.

• Alternatively, if you wish to use a food processor, sift the flour into the bowl of the food processor and add the salt.

• Pour in the eggs and olive oil, add any flavoring, and process until the dough begins to come together.

• Turn out the dough onto a lightly floured counter and knead until smooth. Wrap the dough in plastic wrap and let rest for at least 30 minutes before rolling out or feeding through a pasta machine, as this makes it more elastic. Use as required.

FLAVORED PASTA

TOMATO PASTA: Add 2 tablespoons tomato paste to the flour when making the dough and use 1 1/2 eggs instead of 2.

HERB PASTA: Add 3 tablespoons chopped fresh herbs to the flour.

SPINACH PASTA: Squeeze out as much liquid as possible from 5 1/2 oz/150 g thawed frozen spinach or 8 oz/225 g fresh spinach blanched in boiling water for 1 minute. Chop finely and mix thoroughly with the flour.

WHOLE WHEAT PASTA: Use a scant 1 1/4 cups whole wheat flour sifted with 3 tablespoons white all-purpose flour.

BÉCHAMEL SAUCE

MAKES 1 1/4 CUPS

1 1/4 cups milk
1 bay leaf
6 black peppercorns
slice of onion
mace blade
2 tbsp butter
3 tbsp all-purpose flour
salt and pepper

• Pour the milk into a pan and add the bay leaf, peppercorns, onion, and mace. Heat gently to just below boiling point, then remove from the heat, cover, and let infuse for 10 minutes. Strain the milk into a pitcher.

• Melt the butter in a separate pan. Sprinkle in the flour and cook over low heat, stirring constantly, for 1 minute. Remove from the heat and gradually stir in the milk. Return to the heat and bring to a boil, stirring. Cook, stirring, until thickened and smooth. Season to taste with salt and pepper.

With such a variety of shapes and sizes available, pasta is an extremely versatile food, which lends itself perfectly to many different dishes. It can be served hot or cold, and is not only perfect for main meals but can also be used in numerous delicious soups, appetizers, and light meals, as the recipes in this chapter illustrate.

Some types of pasta are specially designed for soups, as they cook in a short time. These include small rings of anellini, small shells of conchigliette, small butterflies of farfalline, and stars of stelline, along with many more. For children there are small shapes of the alphabet, known as alfabeto, which are always popular. Pasta soups are ideal for using up all those odds and ends of pasta that you have tucked away in the pantry, as in the recipe for White Bean Soup. Get them out now and use them up!

LIGHT FANTASTIC

In Italy, pasta is served as a first course, and although this may seem rather substantial to those not used to it, it is because servings are small and may be followed by a simple broiled fish or meat dish, without numerous accompaniments. Pasta also makes an ideal base for a salad for a perfect light lunch or supper dish. What could be more tempting on a summer's day than a Mediterranean-style salad of griddled fresh tuna steaks, spirals of pasta, green beans, and tomatoes, tossed in a lemony dressing, or pasta shells and charbroiled bell peppers tossed in pesto? It makes your mouth water just thinking about it!

SERVES 8

4 oz/115 g green beans
7 oz/200 g spinach leaves
8 oz/225 g plum tomatoes
2 onions, sliced
2 carrots, diced
2 celery stalks, sliced
2 potatoes, diced
1 cup frozen peas
2 zucchini, diced
3 garlic cloves, sliced
4 tbsp olive oil
8 cups vegetable or chicken stock
5 oz/140 g dried soup pasta
salt and pepper
freshly grated Parmesan cheese, to serve

PESTO

2 garlic cloves
¼ cup pine nuts
4 oz/115 g fresh basil leaves
½ cup freshly grated Parmesan cheese
½ cup olive oil
salt

Genoese Vegetable Soup

Any leftover pesto may be stored in a screw-top jar in the refrigerator for up to two weeks, or used as a sauce for pasta.

• Cut the green beans into 1-inch/2.5-cm lengths. Remove any coarse stalks from the spinach and shred. Peel the tomatoes by cutting a cross in the bottom of each and placing in a heatproof bowl. Cover with boiling water and let stand for 35–45 seconds. Drain and plunge into cold water, then the skins will slide off easily. Seed and dice the tomatoes, then place in a large, heavy-bottom pan together with the onions, carrots, celery, potatoes, peas, zucchini, and garlic. Pour in the olive oil and stock and bring to a boil over medium–low heat. Reduce the heat and let simmer gently for about 1½ hours.

• Meanwhile, make the Pesto. Put the garlic, pine nuts, basil, and a pinch of salt into a mortar and pound to a paste with a pestle. Transfer the mixture to a bowl and gradually work in the Parmesan cheese, using a wooden spoon, followed by the olive oil, to make a thick, creamy sauce. Taste and adjust the seasoning if necessary. Cover with plastic wrap and let chill in the refrigerator until required.

• Season the soup to taste with salt and pepper and add the pasta. Cook for an additional 8–10 minutes, or until the pasta is tender but still firm to the bite. The soup should be very thick. Stir in half the Pesto, remove the pan from the heat, and let stand for 4 minutes. Taste and adjust the seasoning, adding more salt, pepper, and Pesto if necessary. Ladle into warmed bowls and serve immediately. Hand round the grated Parmesan cheese separately.

SERVES 6

2 tbsp olive oil
2 oz/55 g rindless pancetta or lean bacon, diced
2 onions, sliced
2 garlic cloves, finely chopped
3 carrots, chopped
2 celery stalks, chopped
1 cup dried cannellini beans, soaked in cold water to cover overnight
14 oz/400 g canned chopped tomatoes
8 cups beef stock
12 oz/350 g potatoes, diced
6 oz/175 g dried pepe bucato, macaroni, or other soup pasta
6 oz/175 g green beans, sliced
1 cup fresh or frozen peas
8 oz/225 g savoy cabbage, shredded
3 tbsp chopped fresh flat-leaf parsley
salt and pepper
fresh Parmesan cheese shavings, to serve

Minestrone Milanese

It usually takes 1½–2 hours of cooking for soaked cannellini beans to become tender, but this can vary depending on how long they have been stored.

• Heat the olive oil in a large, heavy-bottom pan. Add the pancetta, onions, and garlic and cook, stirring occasionally, for 5 minutes.

• Add the carrots and celery and cook, stirring occasionally, for an additional 5 minutes, or until all the vegetables are softened.

• Drain the soaked beans and add them to the pan with the tomatoes and their can juices and the beef stock. Bring to a boil, then reduce the heat, cover, and let simmer for 1 hour.

• Add the potatoes, re-cover, and cook for 15 minutes, then add the pasta, green beans, peas, cabbage, and parsley. Cover and cook for an additional 15 minutes, or until all the vegetables are tender. Season to taste with salt and pepper. Ladle the soup into warmed soup bowls and serve immediately with Parmesan cheese shavings.

SERVES 4

¾ cup dried cannellini beans, soaked in cold water to cover overnight

1½ quarts chicken or vegetable stock

4 oz/115 g dried corallini, conchigliette piccole, or other soup pasta

6 tbsp olive oil

2 garlic cloves, finely chopped

4 tbsp chopped fresh flat-leaf parsley

salt and pepper

fresh crusty bread, to serve

White Bean Soup

Beans feature widely in Tuscan cuisine. This smooth, comforting soup, in which beans are simmered for 2 hours, is very simple to make. Garlic and parsley, stirred in just before serving, complement the flavor, and a drizzle of olive oil adds the final touch.

- Drain the soaked beans and place them in a large, heavy-bottom pan. Add the stock and bring to a boil. Partially cover the pan, reduce the heat, and let simmer for 2 hours, or until tender.
- Transfer about half the beans and a little of the stock to a food processor or blender and process to a smooth purée. Return the purée to the pan and stir well to mix. Return the soup to a boil.
- Add the pasta to the soup, return to a boil, and cook for 10 minutes, or until tender.
- Meanwhile, heat 4 tablespoons of the olive oil in a small pan. Add the garlic and cook over low heat, stirring frequently, for 4–5 minutes, or until golden. Stir the garlic into the soup and add the parsley. Season to taste with salt and pepper and ladle into warmed soup bowls. Drizzle with the remaining olive oil and serve immediately with crusty bread.

SERVES 4

- 3 tbsp olive oil
- 1 onion, chopped
- 1 red bell pepper, seeded and diced
- 1 orange bell pepper, seeded and diced
- 1 lb 12 oz/800 g canned chopped tomatoes
- 1 tbsp sun-dried tomato paste
- 1 tsp paprika
- 8 oz/225 g pepperoni, sliced
- 2 tbsp chopped fresh flat-leaf parsley, plus extra to garnish
- 1 lb/450 g dried garganelli
- salt and pepper
- mixed salad greens, to serve

Pepperoni Pasta

Pepperoni is a hotly spiced Italian sausage made from pork and beef and flavored with fennel. You could substitute other spicy sausages, such as kabanos or chorizo, if you like. If you cannot find garganelli pasta, then use penne or another pasta shape, such as fusilli, bucati, or farfalle.

• Heat 2 tablespoons of the olive oil in a large, heavy-bottom skillet. Add the onion and cook over low heat, stirring occasionally, for 5 minutes, or until softened. Add the red and orange bell peppers, tomatoes and their can juices, sun-dried tomato paste, and paprika to the pan and bring to a boil.

• Add the pepperoni and parsley and season to taste with salt and pepper. Stir well and bring to a boil, then reduce the heat and simmer for 10–15 minutes.

• Meanwhile, bring a large, heavy-bottom pan of lightly salted water to a boil. Add the pasta, return to a boil, and cook for 8–10 minutes, or until tender but still firm to the bite. Drain well and transfer to a warmed serving dish. Add the remaining olive oil and toss. Add the sauce and toss again. Sprinkle with parsley and serve immediately with mixed salad greens.

SERVES 6

1 potato, diced

14 oz/400 g ground steak

1 onion, finely chopped

1 egg

4 tbsp chopped fresh flat-leaf parsley

all-purpose flour, for dusting

5 tbsp virgin olive oil

1¾ cups strained canned tomatoes

2 tbsp tomato paste

14 oz/400 g dried spaghetti

salt and pepper

TO GARNISH

6 fresh basil leaves, shredded

freshly grated Parmesan cheese

Spaghetti with Meatballs

The humble meatball, served Italian-American style over spaghetti or tagliatelle, is elevated here to greater heights by using fresh ground steak. The meatballs are tender and succulent and enjoyed by both children and adults alike.

• Place the potato in a small pan, add cold water to cover and a pinch of salt, and bring to a boil. Cook for 10–15 minutes until tender, then drain. Either mash thoroughly with a potato masher or fork or pass through a potato ricer.

• Combine the potato, steak, onion, egg, and parsley in a bowl and season to taste with salt and pepper. Spread out the flour on a plate. With dampened hands, shape the meat mixture into walnut-size balls and roll in the flour. Shake off any excess.

• Heat the olive oil in a heavy-bottom skillet, add the meatballs, and cook over medium heat, stirring and turning frequently, for 8–10 minutes, or until golden all over.

• Add the strained tomatoes and tomato paste and cook for an additional 10 minutes, or until the sauce is reduced and thickened.

• Meanwhile, bring a large pan of lightly salted water to a boil. Add the pasta, return to a boil, and cook for 8–10 minutes, or until tender but still firm to the bite.

• Drain well and add to the meatball sauce, tossing well to coat. Transfer to a warmed serving dish, garnish with the basil leaves and grated Parmesan cheese, and serve immediately.

SERVES 4

1½ oz/40 g dried porcini mushrooms
¾ cup hot water
1 lb 12 oz/800 g canned chopped tomatoes
1 fresh red chili, seeded and finely chopped
3 tbsp olive oil
12 oz/350 g skinless, boneless chicken, cut into thin strips
2 garlic cloves, finely chopped
12 oz/350 g dried pappardelle
salt and pepper
2 tbsp chopped fresh flat-leaf parsley, to garnish

Pappardelle with Chicken and Porcini

Wild mushrooms are used extensively in Italian dishes and porcini mushrooms are the most popular. When using porcini, always soak them first in hot water for 30 minutes, then drain well before cooking.

• Place the porcini in a small bowl, add the hot water, and let soak for 30 minutes. Meanwhile, place the tomatoes and their can juices in a heavy-bottom pan and break them up with a wooden spoon, then stir in the chili. Bring to a boil, then reduce the heat and simmer, stirring occasionally, for 30 minutes, or until reduced.

• Remove the mushrooms from their soaking liquid with a slotted spoon, reserving the liquid. Strain the liquid through a coffee filter paper or cheesecloth-lined strainer into the tomatoes and simmer for an additional 15 minutes. Meanwhile, heat 2 tablespoons of the olive oil in a heavy-bottom skillet. Add the chicken and cook, stirring frequently, until golden brown all over and tender. Stir in the mushrooms and garlic and cook for an additional 5 minutes.

• While the chicken is cooking, bring a large, heavy-bottom pan of lightly salted water to a boil. Add the pasta, return to a boil, and cook for 8–10 minutes, or until tender but still firm to the bite. Drain well, then transfer to a warmed serving dish. Drizzle the pasta with the remaining olive oil and toss lightly. Stir the chicken mixture into the tomato sauce, season to taste with salt and pepper, and spoon onto the pasta. Toss lightly, sprinkle with parsley, and serve immediately.

SERVES 4
1 lb/450 g dried spaghetti
1 tbsp olive oil
8 oz/225 g rindless pancetta or lean bacon, chopped
4 eggs
5 tbsp light cream
4 tbsp freshly grated Parmesan cheese
salt and pepper

Spaghetti alla Carbonara

For a more substantial dish, cook 1–2 finely chopped shallots with the pancetta and add 4 oz/115 g sliced mushrooms after 4 minutes, then continue as above.

• Bring a large, heavy-bottom pan of lightly salted water to a boil. Add the pasta, return to a boil, and cook for 8–10 minutes, or until tender but still firm to the bite.

• Meanwhile, heat the olive oil in a heavy-bottom skillet. Add the chopped pancetta and cook over medium heat, stirring frequently, for 8–10 minutes.

• Beat the eggs with the cream in a small bowl and season to taste with salt and pepper. Drain the pasta and return it to the pan. Tip in the contents of the skillet, then add the egg mixture and half the Parmesan cheese. Stir well, then transfer to a warmed serving dish. Serve immediately, sprinkled with the remaining Parmesan cheese.

SERVES 4

- 1 lb/450 g plum tomatoes
- 3 tbsp olive oil
- 2 garlic cloves, finely chopped
- 10 anchovy fillets, drained and chopped
- ¾ cup black olives, pitted and chopped
- 1 tbsp capers, rinsed
- pinch of cayenne pepper
- 14 oz/400 g dried linguine
- salt
- 2 tbsp chopped fresh flat-leaf parsley, to garnish

Linguine alla Puttanesca

Salted anchovies have a much better flavor than canned fillets, but are not so widely available. If you can find them, soak them in cold water for 30 minutes, then pat dry with paper towels before using.

• Peel the tomatoes by cutting a cross in the bottom of each and placing in a heatproof bowl. Cover with boiling water and let stand for 35–45 seconds. Drain and plunge into cold water, then the skins will slide off easily. Seed and chop the tomatoes.

• Heat the olive oil in a heavy-bottom pan. Add the garlic and cook over low heat, stirring frequently, for 2 minutes. Add the anchovies and mash them to a pulp with a fork. Add the olives, capers, and tomatoes and season to taste with cayenne pepper. Cover and let simmer for 25 minutes.

• Meanwhile, bring a pan of lightly salted water to a boil. Add the pasta, return to a boil, and cook for 8–10 minutes, or until tender but still firm to the bite. Drain and transfer to a warmed serving dish.

• Spoon the anchovy sauce into the dish and toss the pasta, using 2 large forks. Garnish with the parsley and serve immediately.

SERVES 4

2 lb 4 oz/1 kg live clams

3/4 cup water

3/4 cup dry white wine

12 oz/350 g dried spaghetti

5 tbsp olive oil

2 garlic cloves, finely chopped

4 tbsp chopped fresh flat-leaf parsley

salt and pepper

Spaghetti with Clams

In Italy, this dish would be prepared with small, smooth-shelled clams, known as vongole, but you can use other varieties, such as cherrystone clams. If fresh clams are not available, substitute with 10 oz/280 g of clams in brine, which are sold in jars.

• Scrub the clams under cold running water and discard any with broken or damaged shells and any that do not shut when sharply tapped. Place the clams in a large, heavy-bottom pan, add the water and wine, cover, and cook over high heat, shaking the pan occasionally, for 5 minutes, or until the shells have opened.

• Remove the clams with a slotted spoon and let cool slightly. Strain the cooking liquid through a cheesecloth-lined strainer into a small pan. Bring to a boil and cook until reduced by about half, then remove from the heat. Meanwhile, discard any clams that have not opened, remove the remainder from their shells, and reserve until required.

• Bring a large pan of lightly salted water to a boil. Add the pasta, return to a boil, and cook for 8–10 minutes, or until tender but still firm to the bite.

• Meanwhile, heat the olive oil in a large, heavy-bottom skillet. Add the garlic and cook, stirring frequently, for 2 minutes. Add the parsley and the reduced clam cooking liquid and let simmer gently.

• Drain the pasta and add it to the skillet with the clams. Season to taste with salt and pepper and cook, stirring constantly, for 4 minutes, or until the pasta is coated and the clams have heated through. Transfer to a warmed serving dish and serve immediately.

SERVES 4

1 lb/450 g dried tagliatelle

salt

fresh basil sprigs, to garnish

PESTO

2 garlic cloves

¼ cup pine nuts

4 oz/115 g fresh basil leaves

½ cup freshly grated Parmesan cheese

½ cup olive oil

salt

Pasta with Pesto

For different flavor variations, try using fresh mint, oregano, or even cilantro in place of the fresh basil leaves in the pesto.

- To make the pesto, put the garlic, pine nuts, a large pinch of salt, and the basil into a mortar and pound to a paste with a pestle. Transfer to a bowl and gradually work in the Parmesan cheese with a wooden spoon, followed by the olive oil, to make a thick, creamy sauce. Taste and adjust the seasoning if necessary.
- Alternatively, put the garlic, pine nuts, and a large pinch of salt into a food processor or blender and process briefly. Add the basil leaves and process to a paste. With the motor still running, gradually add the olive oil. Scrape into a bowl and beat in the Parmesan cheese. Season to taste with salt.
- Bring a large pan of lightly salted water to a boil. Add the pasta, return to a boil, and cook for 8–10 minutes, or until tender but still firm to the bite. Drain the pasta well, return to the pan, and toss with half the pesto, then divide among warmed serving plates and top with the remaining pesto. Garnish the pasta with basil sprigs and serve immediately.

SERVES 4

1 lb/450 g dried spaghetti

½ cup extra virgin olive oil

3 garlic cloves, finely chopped

3 tbsp chopped fresh flat-leaf parsley

salt and pepper

Spaghetti Olio e Aglio

Cooked pasta gets cold quickly, so make sure that the serving dish is warmed thoroughly and as soon as the pasta is drained, transfer to the dish.

• Bring a large, heavy-bottom pan of lightly salted water to a boil. Add the spaghetti, return to a boil, and cook for 8–10 minutes, or until tender but still firm to the bite.

• Meanwhile, heat the olive oil in a heavy-bottom skillet. Add the garlic and a pinch of salt and cook over low heat, stirring constantly, for 3–4 minutes, or until golden. Do not allow the garlic to brown or it will taste bitter. Remove the skillet from the heat.

• Drain the pasta and transfer to a warmed serving dish. Pour in the garlic-flavored olive oil, then add the chopped parsley and season to taste with salt and pepper. Toss well and serve immediately.

SERVES 4

- 4 tbsp butter
- 1 tbsp olive oil
- 6 shallots, sliced
- 1 lb/450 g cremini mushrooms, sliced
- salt and pepper
- 1 tsp all-purpose flour
- 2/3 cup heavy cream or panna da cucina
- 2 tbsp port
- 4 oz/115 g sun-dried tomatoes in oil, drained and chopped
- pinch of freshly grated nutmeg
- 12 oz/350 g dried penne
- 2 tbsp chopped fresh flatleaf parsley

Penne with Creamy Mushrooms

Nutmeg is used widely in Italian cooking as it has a fragrant, sweet aroma. Use freshly grated nutmeg rather than ground, which rapidly deteriorates. Store it in an airtight container.

• Melt the butter with the olive oil in a large heavy-bottom skillet. Add the shallots and cook over low heat, stirring occasionally, for 4–5 minutes, or until softened. Add the mushrooms and cook for an additional 2 minutes. Season to taste with salt and pepper, then sprinkle in the flour and cook, stirring, for 1 minute.

• Remove the skillet from the heat and gradually stir in the cream and port. Return to the heat, add the sun-dried tomatoes and grated nutmeg, and cook over low heat, stirring occasionally, for 8 minutes.

• Meanwhile, bring a large heavy-bottom pan of lightly salted water to a boil. Add the pasta, return to a boil, and cook for 8–10 minutes, or until tender but still firm to the bite. Drain well and add to the mushroom sauce. Cook for 3 minutes, then transfer to a warmed serving dish. Sprinkle with the chopped parsley and serve immediately.

SERVES 4

- 12 oz/350 g dried fusilli
- 3 tbsp olive oil
- 12 oz/350 g wild mushrooms or white mushrooms, sliced
- 1 garlic clove, finely chopped
- 1¾ cups heavy cream
- 9 oz/250 g Gorgonzola cheese, crumbled
- salt and pepper
- 2 tbsp chopped fresh flat-leaf parsley, to garnish

Fusilli with Gorgonzola and Mushroom Sauce

Wild mushrooms have a much earthier flavor than cultivated ones, so they complement the strong taste of the cheese. Porcini are especially delicious, but rather expensive. Portobello mushrooms would also be a good choice. Otherwise, use cultivated mushrooms, but add 1 oz/25 g dried porcini, soaked for 30 minutes in 1 cup hot water.

• Bring a large pan of lightly salted water to a boil. Add the pasta, return to a boil, and cook for 8–10 minutes, or until tender but still firm to the bite.

• Meanwhile, heat the olive oil in a heavy-bottom pan. Add the mushrooms and cook over low heat, stirring frequently, for 5 minutes. Add the garlic and cook for an additional 2 minutes.

• Add the cream, bring to a boil, and cook for 1 minute until slightly thickened. Stir in the cheese and cook over low heat until it has melted. Do not allow the sauce to boil once the cheese has been added. Season to taste with salt and pepper and remove the pan from the heat.

• Drain the pasta and tip it into the sauce. Toss well to coat, then serve immediately, garnished with the parsley.

SERVES 4

2/3 cup dry white wine
1 tbsp sun-dried tomato paste
2 fresh red chilies
2 garlic cloves, finely chopped
12 oz/350 g dried tortiglioni
4 tbsp chopped fresh flat-leaf parsley
salt and pepper
fresh romano cheese shavings, to garnish

SUGOCASA

5 tbsp extra virgin olive oil
1 lb/450 g plum tomatoes, chopped
salt and pepper

Hot Chili Pasta

If time is short, use ready-made sugocasa, which is available from specialty stores, sometimes labeled "crushed tomatoes." You could also use strained canned tomatoes, but the sauce will be thinner.

• First make the sugocasa. Heat the olive oil in a skillet until it is almost smoking. Add the tomatoes and cook over high heat for 2–3 minutes. Reduce the heat to low and cook gently for 20 minutes, or until very soft. Season with salt and pepper, then pass through a food mill or blender into a clean pan.
• Add the wine, sun-dried tomato paste, whole chilies, and garlic to the sugocasa and bring to a boil. Reduce the heat and simmer gently.
• Meanwhile, bring a large pan of lightly salted water to a boil. Add the pasta, return to a boil, and cook for 8–10 minutes, or until tender but still firm to the bite.
• Meanwhile, remove the chilies and taste the sauce. If you prefer a hotter flavor, chop some or all of the chilies and return them to the pan. Check the seasoning at the same time, then stir in half the parsley.
• Drain the pasta and tip it into a warmed serving bowl. Add the sauce and toss to coat. Sprinkle with the remaining parsley, garnish with the romano shavings, and serve immediately.

The majority of baked pasta dishes, the two most well known perhaps being lasagna and macaroni and cheese, have one thing in common, which is that the ingredients are prepared or cooked separately and then assembled in the dish just before baking in the oven. Pasta, other ingredients such as meat, cheese, or vegetables, and a sauce are the typical components. One part of these dishes that you will need time and time again is Béchamel Sauce and so it has been included on page 6 for easy reference.

The Italians even have a name for these baked dishes—it is called pasticci. Many baked pasta dishes are traditional dishes, since pasticci were often served at banquets as far back as the eighteenth century. In those days they were known as timballi, but today the word timballo is used to describe a baked dish that is served turned out of its dish.

BAKED TO PERFECTION

These baked pasta dishes are substantial and are therefore suitable for serving as a main meal. They are also ideal for buffet parties when feeding a large number of people, as they are easy to serve and can be eaten with just a fork. An additional advantage is that they can be prepared in advance. All that is needed to accompany them is a fresh green salad.

SERVES 4

- 3 tbsp olive oil
- 1 onion, finely chopped
- 1 celery stalk, finely chopped
- 1 carrot, finely chopped
- 3½ oz/100 g pancetta or rindless lean bacon, finely chopped
- 6 oz/175 g ground beef
- 6 oz/175 g ground pork
- generous ⅓ cup dry red wine
- ⅔ cup beef stock
- 1 tbsp tomato paste
- 1 clove
- 1 bay leaf
- ⅔ cup boiling milk
- 14 oz/400 g dried lasagna
- 4 tbsp unsalted butter, diced, plus extra for greasing
- 1¼ cups Béchamel Sauce
- 5 oz/140 g mozzarella cheese, diced
- 1¼ cups freshly grated Parmesan cheese
- salt and pepper

Baked Lasagna

This classic Italian dish is a specialty of the Emilia-Romagna region, the gastronomic center of Italy. It can be made with dried or fresh lasagna and either verde (spinach) or egg lasagna. You could also use all ground beef or all ground pork if wished.

• Heat the olive oil in a large, heavy-bottom pan. Add the onion, celery, carrot, pancetta, beef, and pork and cook over medium heat, stirring frequently and breaking up the meat with a wooden spoon, for 10 minutes, or until lightly browned.

• Add the wine, bring to a boil, and cook until reduced. Add about two-thirds of the stock, bring to a boil, and cook until reduced. Combine the remaining stock and tomato paste and add to the pan. Season to taste with salt and pepper, add the clove and bay leaf, and pour in the milk. Cover and let simmer over a low heat for 1½ hours.

• Preheat the oven to 400°F/200°C. Unless you are using lasagna that needs no precooking, bring a large, heavy-bottom pan of lightly salted water to a boil. Add the lasagna sheets, in batches, return to a boil, and cook for about 10 minutes, or until tender but still firm to the bite. Remove with tongs and spread out on a clean dish towel. Remove the meat sauce from the heat and discard the clove and bay leaf.

• Lightly grease a large, ovenproof dish with butter. Place a layer of lasagna in the bottom and cover it with a layer of meat sauce. Spoon a layer of Béchamel Sauce on top and sprinkle with one-third of the mozzarella and Parmesan cheeses. Continue making layers until all the ingredients are used, ending with a topping of Béchamel Sauce and sprinkled cheese.

• Dot the top of the lasagna with the diced butter and bake in the preheated oven for 30 minutes, or until golden and bubbling.

SERVES 4

2 tbsp olive oil
1 onion, chopped
1 garlic clove, finely chopped
2 carrots, diced
2 oz/55 g pancetta or rindless lean bacon, chopped
4 oz/115 g mushrooms, chopped
1 lb/450 g ground pork
½ cup dry white wine
4 tbsp strained canned tomatoes
7 oz/200 g canned chopped tomatoes
2 tsp chopped fresh sage or ½ tsp dried sage
8 oz/225 g dried elicoidali
5 oz/140 g mozzarella cheese, diced
4 tbsp freshly grated Parmesan cheese
1¼ cups hot Béchamel Sauce
salt and pepper

Pork and Pasta Bake

When cooking with olive oil, there is no need to use extra virgin olive oil as the flavor will be lost during cooking. Olive oil is best stored in a cool place, out of direct sunlight. Do not store in the refrigerator.

• Preheat the oven to 400°F/200°C. Heat the olive oil in a large, heavy-bottom skillet. Add the onion, garlic, and carrots and cook over low heat, stirring occasionally, for 5 minutes, or until the onion has softened. Add the pancetta and cook for 5 minutes. Add the chopped mushrooms and cook, stirring occasionally, for an additional 2 minutes. Add the pork and cook, breaking it up with a wooden spoon, until the meat is browned all over. Stir in the wine, strained tomatoes, chopped tomatoes and their can juices, and sage. Season to taste with salt and pepper and bring to a boil, then cover and simmer over low heat for 25–30 minutes.

• Meanwhile, bring a large, heavy-bottom pan of lightly salted water to a boil. Add the pasta, return to a boil, and cook for 8–10 minutes, or until tender but still firm to the bite.

• Spoon the pork mixture into a large ovenproof dish. Stir the mozzarella and half the Parmesan cheese into the Béchamel Sauce. Drain the pasta and stir the sauce into it, then spoon it over the pork mixture. Sprinkle with the remaining Parmesan cheese and bake in the oven for 25–30 minutes, or until golden brown. Serve immediately.

SERVES 4

12 dried cannelloni tubes
4 tbsp olive oil, plus extra for brushing
2 tbsp butter
1 lb/450 g mixed wild mushrooms, finely chopped
1 garlic clove, finely chopped
1½ cups fresh bread crumbs
2/3 cup milk
1 cup ricotta cheese
6 tbsp freshly grated Parmesan cheese
2 tbsp pine nuts
2 tbsp slivered almonds
salt and pepper

TOMATO SAUCE

2 tbsp olive oil
1 onion, finely chopped
1 garlic clove, finely chopped
1 lb 12 oz/800 g canned chopped tomatoes
1 tbsp tomato paste
8 black olives, pitted and chopped
salt and pepper

Mushroom Cannelloni

Use either a teaspoon or a pastry bag fitted with a large plain tip to fill the cannelloni tubes. Do not overfill them.

• Preheat the oven to 375°F/190°C. Bring a large pan of lightly salted water to a boil. Add the cannelloni tubes, return to a boil, and cook for 8–10 minutes, or until tender but still firm to the bite. With a slotted spoon, transfer the cannelloni tubes to a plate and pat dry. Brush a large ovenproof dish with olive oil.

• Meanwhile, make the Tomato Sauce. Heat the olive oil in a skillet. Add the onion and garlic and cook over low heat for 5 minutes, or until softened. Add the tomatoes and their can juices, tomato paste, and olives and season to taste with salt and pepper. Bring to a boil and cook for 3–4 minutes. Pour the sauce into the ovenproof dish.

• To make the filling, melt the butter in a heavy-bottom skillet. Add the mushrooms and garlic and cook over medium heat, stirring frequently, for 3–5 minutes, or until tender. Remove the skillet from the heat. Mix the bread crumbs, milk, and olive oil together in a large bowl, then stir in the ricotta, mushroom mixture, and 4 tablespoons of the Parmesan cheese. Season to taste with salt and pepper.

• Fill the cannelloni tubes with the mushroom mixture and place them in the dish. Brush with olive oil and sprinkle with the remaining Parmesan cheese, pine nuts, and almonds. Bake in the oven for 25 minutes, or until golden.